COLUMBIA COLLEGE CHICAGO

W9-DJO-049

THE POETICS OF RAGE

COLUMBIA COLLEGE LIBRARY
600 S. MICHIGAN AVENUE
CHICAGO, IL 60605

Wole Soyinka, Jean Toomer, and Claude McKay

Emmanuel E. Egar

University Press of America,® Inc.
Lanham · Boulder · New York · Toronto · Oxford

ENTERED DEC 1 4 2005

Copyright © 2005 by
University Press of America,® Inc.
4501 Forbes Boulevard
Suite 200
Lanham, Maryland 20706
UPA Acquisitions Department (301) 459-3366

PO Box 317
Oxford
OX2 9RU, UK

All rights reserved
Printed in the United States of America
British Library Cataloging in Publication Information Available

Library of Congress Control Number: 2005921304
ISBN 0-7618-3150-9 (paperback : alk. ppr.)

⊖™ The paper used in this publication meets the minimum
requirements of American National Standard for Information
Sciences—Permanence of Paper for Printed Library Materials,
ANSI Z39.48—1984

Dedication

This text is dedicated to my beloved uncle,
Michael Nlang Ebine, who, like Gorgias of Leotini,
introduced my early life to the Magic of Words.

Contents

vi

Preface

There is truth, a universal truth, an axiom of faith that every human being has that propensity to resist humiliation and the pain that comes out of it. Usually the literary artist, the conscience of his society, is at the forefront of that agitation. That is why Wole Soyinka, a Nigerian poet across the Atlantic Ocean; Claude McKay and Jean Toomer, both American poets, used their works to express their rage, their frustrating anxiety, doubt, hope and even desire about humiliation. Their rage and bitterness filter out in fountains and cadences in their use of language.

In terms of language, each poet followed the advice of the ancient critic Horace, that a writer must use language suitable for his theme to enunciate that theme. That is why Soyinka uses the metaphor of decay, filth and rottenness to reveal the political perversions in Nigeria. McKay does the same in most of his poems, particularly in "If We Must Die". Toomer does the same in "Georgia Dusk". This text deals with that universal attitude to pain—the pain of discrimination, whether in tribalism, political corruption or institutional legal terrorism.

Introduction

The theme of this text is found in that insinuation of Wole Soyinka's artistic credo in his essay "The Writer in a Modern African State." In this warm and animated essay, Soyinka claims that

> When the writer in his own society can no longer function as conscience, he must recognize that his choice lies between denying himself totally or withdrawing to the position of chronicler and post mortem surgeon (20).

This text deals with how each of these poets interpreted their roles as the conscience and protector of that conscience in their societies. How each writer has taken on the self-imposed mantle of priest, prophet and poet in their dealings with the frustrations, anxieties, doubts, hopes and desires of each society. It deals with how each of these poets used poetry, a medium of the diviners, the prophet and the priest, almost with religious veneration, to shape the morals and conscience of their society. It deals with how these poets saw their voices as the voice of God, and how *Vox Populi* became *Vox dei*. The text deals with the universal miasma of political pain and how to resist it.

Chapter I

An Appreciation of the Preface to "A Shuttle in the Crypt"

Wole Soyinka is one of the most renowned, prolific writers of English Literature in the world today. As poet and dramatist, his rich and enormous contribution to the field was rewarded in 1986. That was the year he won the coveted Nobel Prize in literature and the first black person from the African continent to ever win that prize. The selection of poems from this combustive, tension-packed title, "A Shuttle in the Crypt," may have been written between 1968 and 1971, a period when the poet was mentally and physically brutalized through imprisonment for daring to exercise his freedom of speech. And as we all know, the human speech is perhaps the worst enemy of a dictatorship. To appreciate these poems, we must start from the rather curious title "A Shuttle in the Crypt."

This title seems to animate the tension, the combustion, the fire and fury, the frustration, anxiety, doubt, hope and even desire of the happy, vibrant poet who was forcefully cut from human contact in an attempt to break the human spirit. This is how the poet describes it:

> The Shuttle is a unique species of the caged animal, a restless bolt of energy, a trapped weaverbird, yet charged in repose with unspoken forms and designs. In motion as in rest it is a secretive seed, shrine, kernel, phallus and well of creative mysteries (7).

In this piece, the metaphor of the poet as the weaverbird (a bird charged with eternal clarion calls) but cut, trapped and isolated from all human contact, breeds a tendency to unleash nothing but flaming fury. That fury would be the logical outcome because this weaverbird (this musician, this preacher) even in repose, is still charged with unspoken forms and designs.

But these unspoken forms and designs soon take on other metaphors: metonymy, synecdoche, catachresis and even presopopaiea with all their vibrant nuances of negation/affirmation which make Wole Soyinka a chemist or an alchemist of English poetic language when he writes, "In motion or at rest it is a secretive seed, shrine, kernel, phallus and well of creative mysteries" (7).

Here we witness how Soyinka, the chemist of English language, carefully selects words like a chemist dispenses medications. Words that have reactions and vibrations that spread like a contagion to unleash endless significations. A reader can embrace his restrained fury in the secretive "seed" with its life giving attributes, the "shrine," an alter for religious rituals of appeasement, consolation and plea. In this metaphor of the "shrine," the physical isolation takes on a hidden metaphysical poetic conceit in the sense that the isolation of the poet now takes on a religious experience. The experience is that the shrine, as an alter for religious rituals, should stay open for religious practices by the community of believers and not caged or locked away, thereby depriving the believers this sanctuary for worship. The "kernel" is a seed from a West African palm tree. It is a small seed, but it gives birth to tall towering palm trees that produce wine and oil for cooking food. A life-giving seed! And the male organ "Phallus," a symbol of procreation, regeneration, continuity, contiguity and the preserver of human history, seems to thrive better in an atmosphere of freedom than restriction and isolation. A man in solitary confinement without any form of human contact cannot have a family. This restriction is another way to kill humanity as well as creativity. Soyinka, the poet/dramatist, sees himself in these muted metaphors, this alchemy of creative energy which if restricted will ruin not only the poet, but also the creative genesis of the human race. In evoking this mood, this sense of irreparable loss to society, Soyinka should remind the reader of John Keats in his poem "When I Have Fears That I May Cease To Be." In this poem, Keats moans about the fact that early death will prevent him from reaching his poetic achievements. But somehow, in a tone of self-righteousness he seemed to be concerned more about what the world would lose as a result of his early death than his personal demise. Soyinka, like John Keats, seemed to be concerned here not so much about his restriction, but with the enormous loss to the world of creativity resulting from his restriction.

The poet then reveals the haunting genesis of these poems which were written at a period of cruel solitary confinement. He gives the reader an anatomy of the characteristics of a brutal incarceration in,

> It is the map of the course trodden by the mind, not record of actual struggle against a vegetable existence. (vii)

His records in these poems are landscapes or documentation of the tedious path of a haunting nostalgia of memory. The metaphysical conceit in the metaphor of memory as a "map," moves the discourse from the physical vegetation to the human mind. But yet, this metaphor retains the richness of usage both in the physical world and in the realm of human experience. This metaphor serves the same role as the metaphor of the elephant in a fable who does not simply serve a poetic or metonymic function, but enriches the discourse by its very presence. And the poignancy of this punishment for the poet was that he was on the receiving side so that he could not fight back. The poet then attempts to explain the genesis of various titles of poems such as "Chimes of Silence," "Bearings," and "Phases of Peril."

Soyinka claims that the poems under the title of "Chimes of Silence" are central to the whole haunting experience of forced isolation in prison because these poems enunciate the anatomy and horror of watching condemned men move daily to their death by hanging. This awful experience, the poet explains, in a subdued tone of oxymoron and pathos __ that it was harrowing and consoling. Harrowing because when one human being watches a human execution, hanging, that person spiritually, emotionally and physically cannot help but anticipate the frailty of his own mortality. This dreadful experience becomes paradoxically consoling because death is swift and terminal with its blinding finality. That was why when the poet witnessed this constant hanging (enactment of death in the house of death) even the energy (restive and pensive) in the caged bird begins to wane and finally gives room to blistering fury and rage. In this documentation of torture and humiliation, the details of the landscape are different, but the trauma of human pain remains the same with all its horror, mutilation, agony, desperation, doubts, with all their binding sanctifications. The poems under the title "Bearings" are a depiction of physical details, while in "Phases of Peril," the poem, "Conversation at Night," is there only to evoke the pathos of pessimism.

In a tone of subdued rage, the poet laments that while physical punishment could be tolerated, the most brutally destructive thing to do to another human being is to deprive him of human contact. But in the mind of the dictator and the twisted-minded butchers, their hope was to break the human spirit through physical deprivation. Sadly, they were attacking the wrong place in the human anatomy. They should have attacked the mind instead of the body. Wole Soyinka's poems in these selections depict the horrors of solitary confinement. They should remind us of the wisdom of Roland Barthes when he hinted that in a period of moral and political perversion, the writer is the only person inflicted with the gift of "bad conscience."

Chapter II

Wole Soyinka: Poetic Influences

Vladimir Nabokov, the Russian Literary Scholar wrote a warm and animating text on the masterpieces of Western European novels. In his text, *Lectures on Literature,* Nabokov discussed the masterpieces of Western European literature. Nabokov informs us that in literary writings, "the old talent always prefers the safety of their place in history," while the young seem to "shoot to exploit the sky." Nabokov is the only writer that I know who is able to locate the critical genesis of inspiration and writing. That inspiration comes from two Russian words, "vostorg" which means rapture and "udokhovenie," which means recapture. He claims that every form of quality writing comes from that gush of inspiration in the form of rapture. The writer then recaptures this rapture through the enunciation of his frustrations, anxieties, doubts, hopes and even desires. This is how the masters move their modes of enunciation from association to dissociation.

Soyinka's inspiration, his rapture from the poems treated in this text comes from his political incarceration. Through physical restriction and isolation, the movement of the human body is restricted, but the mind is untouched. This restriction further intensifies the inspiration of the mind because it is left to nourish and roam fertile grounds in search of endless significations. But in Soyinka's attempt to recapture his rapture (his inspiration) as a poet, the question that has usually plagued us is "Who are his poetic ancestral influences?" We do not know. So, we can only speculate. It may come from his origin. He is Yoruba, a tribe in Nigeria, with a language rich in metaphors, metonymy, synecdoche and catachresis. It may also come from the mythical Yoruba god, Ogun, the god of creation and destruction, of affirmation and negation. It maybe from this influence that in his poetry, words seem to have built-in tensions of affirmation and negation with all their nuances of endless significations.

In our search for poetic ancestral influences we must consult Harold Bloom, in his text, *The Anxiety of Influence*, and W. Jackson Bate and his text *The Burden of the Past and the English Poet*. Both writers deal with the seeming frustrations of poets who have to struggle with the anxieties of competing with the masterpieces of their predecessors and ancestors. Bloom asserts that no poet can claim to be original; that every form of writing is an imitation, a mimesis of previous works. But his deadly claim is that some writers metaphorically kill their predecessors (the Oedipus Complex) so as to build on the ashes of their temples. Here is where he fell victim to Terry Eagleton's fierce and combative ridicule and polemics, which to me, in this instance, seems to stray too far from literature to the politics of the right and left wing religious sectarianism.

However, if Bloom informs us that modern writers are obsessed with imitation of their predecessors, Bate in his text *The Burden of the Past and the English Poet* has a different view on this rhetoric of influences between the moderns and the ancient. In this text, Bate informs us of the anxieties of poets who had to compete with the masterpieces of masters like Homer, Sophocles, Dante, Shakespeare, Goethe and Dickens. But the transitions of modes or thematic enunciations had no militant or repressive tendencies. It is true however, that poets like John Keats, Dryden, Goethe and Eliot had their anxieties. And we can see these anxieties as they unfolded. Keats, in his letter to his friend Richard Woodhouse on October 27, 1818, remarked that "There was nothing original to be written in poetry; that its riches were already exhausted— and all its beauties forestalled (5)". This is the moaning of a man who seems to lack self-confidence, creativity or is simply overwhelmed by the enormity of the accomplishments of his predecessors. And we remember Goethe's celebrated relief and excitement that he was not born an Englishman, so that he would not struggle and confront the masterpieces. He shares his luck with us when he claims that

> But had I been born an Englishman, and had the manifold master-pieces pressed in upon me, with all their power from my first youthful awakening, it would have overwhelmed me and I would not have known what I wanted to do. I would never have been able to advance with so light and cheerful a spirit, but would certainly have been obligated to consider for a long time and look about me in order to find some new expedient. (6).

Goethe writes in this piece as if literature was bound and restricted to national boundaries and language. He forgot the endless compass of Shakespeare's universal ideas. Ideas that cover almost all the pervasive human problems of anxiety, frustration, doubts, hopes and even desires that Shakespeare manipulated and mastered. He forgot that Shakespeare covered issues that span every area of human habitation and the universe of ideas. How could he escape these areas, particularly if there were accurate English translations in German. It is however interesting to note that Goethe in that piece shows no form of hostility or violence towards Shakespeare. What we find is respect, relief and the need to chart unused grounds for artistic performance. T.S. Eliot also expressed anxiety but showed supreme respect for the poetry of his predecessors or even ancestors. He claims that "Not only every great poet, but every genuine though lesser poet fulfills once for all some possibility of language and so leaves one possibility less for his successor (4)." It is difficult to surmise what aspect of language Eliot refers to. Does he mean the exhaustion in terms of style, the use of English idioms or other precarious modes of enunciation? But it was the same Eliot who later gave such flowering praise for the poetry of metaphysical poets. He informs us that "Metaphysical poets are the prototype of genuine English tradition from which poetry has since strayed."(22). The richness of metaphysical poetry that Eliot refers to deals with the rich use of conceit. A style and wit in idiom where a word in the poem is fused with tensions of affirmation/ negation with diverse forms of significations. And this is the use of wit in all the rich and varied senses that Louis Martz refers to as "intellect, reason, powerful mental capacity, cleverness, ingenuity, intellectual quickness, inventive and constructive ability, a talent for uttering brilliant things and the power of amusing surprise." (*Introduction to 17th Century Poetry.* 1).

But none of these poets from Keats, Goethe, Eliot, Dryden and Pope showed any form of hostility, negation or repressive tendencies toward their predecessor, ancestors or ancients. What the major poets did, according to Bate, was simply tried to find out what their predecessors had left out and so capitalized on it. Dryden for instance, saw that Shakespeare had not used rhyme in dramatic tragedy and so decided to exploit it. And there were several praises by English poets for their predecessors and even ancestors. We see this in Charles Gildon, who wrote an essay in 1449 on "For the Modern Poets Against the Ancients," where he described the new spirit of strict regulation and analysis as more "essential

to poetry than any other form of art or science (24)." Dryden did not
quarrel with any of these tributes. Nor did Pope when William Guthrie
boasted on dramatic poetry, particularly tragedy, where he claimed that
"It at least stands upon the same footing as our noble system of Newtonian
Philosophy." The Newtonian Philosophy he referred to was the love of
formal ideas of order and decorum and that warm "Shaftsburian benevo-
lence." It is of interest to note that even Alexander Pope, the great sati-
rist, did not criticize Guthrie. And Dryden, among the English poets,
knew that his predecessors had exhausted every human humor, character
or plot. But he did not criticize them for that. Instead, he accepted their
achievements nobly because "We acknowledge them our fathers who
had already spent their estates before these came to their children (26)."
In a tone of subdued exasperation he leaves the reader with paradoxical
choices: either not to write at all or to attempt other ways. So, in none of
these expressions of anxiety has any English poet been openly hostile to
his predecessor or repressive of their achievements that Bloom wrote in
his book *The Anxiety of Influence*.

However, from Jackson Bate, we learn the history of the genealogy
of Western European history of ideas. And how each master-poet dealt
with influences of his predecessors or how he/she sometimes leap-frogged
to ancestral grounds to find out unexploited areas so as to build their
castles. From critical observation, it is easy to speculate that Soyinka's
poetic lineage are metaphysical poets with all their rich conceit that he
uses so luxuriously.

Soyinka uses the modes, techniques and enunciations of metaphysi-
cal poets to dramatize his anxieties, frustrations, doubts, hopes and de-
sires that deal with modern decadence in moral, politics and even spiri-
tual spheres. His poetry seems to be a mutation of the ancestral and the
modern techniques and themes. But, to fully understand these warm in-
fluences, we must scan the major characteristics of metaphysical po-
etry to see why he used them.

Essentially, the major characteristics of metaphysical poetry, according
to Louis Martz, in his *Introduction to the 17th Century Poetry*, include

1. That they seem to begin in the midst of an occasion and the
   meaning of the occasion is explored and grasped through
   this particular use of metaphor.
2. Metaphysical poets tend to use old Renaissance Conceit. In
   this, the ingenious comparison is developed into a device by

which the extremes of abstraction and concreteness, extremes of unlikeliness maybe woven together into a fabric of argument that is unified by the prevailing force of wit.

3. They dealt with abrupt openings and use of conversational speech found in "Wyatt, Sidney and Ben Johnson."
4. They dealt with introspection and self-analysis seems mostly in Dunne and Herbert.
5. They dealt with meditation: "A movement from composition of place, into the three fold movement of memory, understanding and will. The meditative art is as changing, resourceful and elusive as the mind in which the meditation is enacted (2)."

As we meditate on metaphysical poetry, I have a belief almost superstitious that one should never complete a text on style without consulting some of that very rich wisdom from Roland Barthes. So, I was driven naturally to his essay on "Style as Craftsmanship." In this warm and interesting text, Barthes teaches us that it was Flaubert,

> Who most methodically laid the foundations for this conception of writing as a craft. (64)

Flaubert inherited bourgeois writing "Style." A style which emphasized rigidity, strictness, order and decorum with a thought that was so transparent because essentially stereotypical and because language was common property of the society. Flaubert saw the deficiencies and artificialities of bourgeois style. He accepted this style, but worked through it to create a novelty. That novelty was to write in such a way that his writing, through its order, decorum and strictness, critically turned its attention to its obvious artificialities. This is language that mocks itself so as to create an improvement.

Barthes goes on to show us the genealogy of the masters of craftsmanship in French Literature. Some of these masters include Gautier, the past master of belles letters; Flaubert, grinding away at his sentences at Croisset; Valery in his room early in the morning working on his craft, his form, and André Gide, standing at his desk like a carpenter, applying nuts and bolts to his craft. And like a genius who writes because the wants to educate, enchant and even edify, Barthes teaches us that:

Flaubertization of writing redeems all writers at a stroke, partly be-
cause the least exacting abandon themselves to it without qualms, and
partly because the purest return to it as to an acknowledgement of their
fate. (66).

Soyinka, like Flaubert accepts the metaphysical poetic style as a craft
with all its artificialities and deficiencies. But he works through irony,
satire and sarcasm. And we know that sarcasm and irony have the capac-
ity to break an argument, an idea or thought to bits and pieces. That is
why Soyinka uses conceit and wit to ridicule and mock metaphysical
style through that curious juxtaposition of the sacred over the profane
that we see in "The Wailing Wall" and "Purgatorio."

Chapter III

The Wailing Wall

The poem "The Wailing Wall" has a muted and fused metaphysical conceit because it immediately instigates a curiosity as well as evokes an aura of the religious—the sacred on the profane. This symbolic as well as metonymic significance of the metaphor needs an explanation.

"The Wailing Wall" is an enclosed area in Jerusalem near the mosque of Omar. This area is supposed to contain the stones of King Solomon's temple where Jews gather every Friday to worship and lament. But "The Wailing Wall" in the prison is a physical wall which separates the prison cell of the poet from that of condemned men waiting to be executed. Soyinka, like a typical metaphysical poet, introduces a poetic conceit into the title of the poem. This conceit resides in the sense that this ordinary wall in the cell of a prison is conferred with religious veneration that makes it synonymous with the holy Wailing Wall in Jerusalem. The ironic twist here is that while "The Wailing Wall" in Jerusalem is a sacred place reserved for prayer of atonement by the living, the prison wall serves another purpose. It is a place of sacrilege and sin, where condemned men are constantly cursing as well as waiting for death. The conceit is in the ironic twist of using language to provoke an aura of the sacred over the profane.

The beauty of Soyinka's poetic conceit in the title of this poem should immediately remind the reader of that beautiful essay by Emmanuel Levinas on Michel Leiris's "Biffures." In this essay, Levinas refers particularly to the richness of the association of ideas whose latent birth Leiris describes so warmly. Leiris's critical talent according to Levinas was in "his association of ideas due to their organic brotherhood, by using thought simply as symbols (145)." This quote means that in this work, one thought seems to feed naturally into another. Levinas informs us that this peculiar style was reflected in the treatment of Rimbaud's famous Sonnet. In his treatment of this sonnet, the correspondences that Leiris provoked were no longer mysterious. This is so because the thought provoked could be easily traced back to its genesis in the sense that "thought deletes itself creating a vacuum that seizes thought at the privileged moment at which it turns into something other than itself (145)."

Soyinka, like Michel Lieris, uses similar style, a similar capacity to use thought simply as symbols. That is why, when the symbol of "The Wailing Wall" is evoked, it is no longer mysterious because the thought could be traced back to its genesis, the Wailing Wall in Jerusalem, a sacred spot containing the stones of Solomon's temple, where Orthodox Jews pray and lament each Friday.

This poem is an anatomy, a dramatization of the ritual of death. In the poem, we witness the gathering of birds of prey, birds of vermin such as vultures, the crow and scavengers all summoned to attend to this ritual of death. The poem opens with

> Wall to polar star, wall of prayers
> A roof in blood-rust floats beyond
> Stained-glass wounds on wailing walls
> Vulture presides in tattered surplice
> In schism for collection plates, with . . . (34).

Everything in this stanza provokes that aura of the sacred over the profane. There is that bitter irony, like a dance of death, where the ugly is juxtaposed to the beautiful, the affirmative over negation, synthesis over antithesis—all of which are calculated to intensify the ugliness of the situation. There is this "wall to polar star," reminiscent of the Jewish reverence for the Star of David and the sacred wall of prayers. But this seemingly holy wall has a roof in blood rust over it. This wall also contains stain glass wounds. And there is this almost unbearable, ominous insinuation of the vulture, a bird of decay, of filth, rottenness, and death. And this bitter joke is no longer funny when this vulture, this bird of decay presides over the sacred on the profane creating a terrible schism reminiscent of scriptural prohibition to avoid adding new wine to an old skin.

This vulture emerges because of the smell of death. There is an appearance of another bird of vermin; a bird of prey (the crow) with a "white collar" like a preacher in the church and legs of "toothpick dearth" that plunges into wasting, decaying meat. The crow is like a choirmaster who conducts a hymn with discordant notes. Here, the poet invokes prayers to a god who has already been disobeyed: "Invocation to broken word on broken voices." The poet seems to wonder here how these sinful prayers could expect any form of salvation. They cannot. Instead of blessings, these people will receive "air tramp, black verger on dry prayers" to altars of evil, where the victims rather their tormentors seem to give charity, rather than receive it. And in a self-righteous tone, the poet admonishes these perpetuators of evil, warning them that the Lord may not receive their prayers if they do not repent their ways.

> On your raft of faith, calling
> Darkness dawn to nightfall
> I fear in vain your exorcise the past
> For evil is impertinent, evil feeds
> Upon wounds and tears of piety.

We see here their precarious faith like a raft, floating on dangerous waters. Even the day breeds only darkness to nightfall. The prayers of these evil people take on the role of a witch doctor calling on the demonic spirits of the past for blessings. But this cannot be because evil respects neither person nor rules. That is why evil seems to "feed on wounds" and "tears of pity." And there is an invocation to this wall, a personification that seems to transcend the wall to God, Almighty, Himself. The poet seems to invoke the power of this wall an (appeal really to God) to look into himself to discover the evil that has been perpetuated. This seems like a plea to God to wake up and see the atrocities committed in His name. Only in this way can God stop future evils because right before God's eyes evil continues to flourish and mount.

> Oh wall of prayer, preyed up
> By scavenge, undertaker.
>
> Nightly the plough
> Furrows deep in graveyards of the sky
> For a mass burial
> Before the lowering poised
> A long coffin of the roof

Bulks against the sky—
Glow of mounting candles in far spaces.

These lines are an appeal to the wall that transports it to God, Himself, who is reminded to watch the profanity committed against Him by evil men. Because how could God not be moved by these wanton evils where men are buried daily in mass graves with very little human veneration? In a tone of sober but desperate submission, the poet watches this human decadence as the "Clouds drift across the Plough. The shore is sunk and hope buried in soil of darkness."

The sense of rage here is relayed through a religious experience, where man seems to display a morality of dog-eat-dog, while at the same time hypocritically calling on God even in his sin. The rage is in that self-controlled anger when one man is confronted with a power beyond his capacity. This is the kind of poetry that meets the defined criteria of metaphysical poetry that Louis Martz refers to in his introduction: "Poetry is metaphysical when it seeks by complex analogies to find a central principle of being within the bounds of a given situation (2)". The central principle of being here should be quite clear and short, if we do not intend to plunge into theological discourse about the goodness of God and the ontological argument. Suffice to say that, the central principle of being is that since God made man in his own image and likeness, he expects man to act right and follow in God's footsteps. And Soyinka uses various analogies to challenge this central principle of being. We see this when he evokes that aura of the sacred "Wailing Wall" on the profane sacrilege of the wall in prison. We witness it in the morality of the dog-eat-dog perpetuated between man and man. We see it in the lack of empathy, ethos/pathos in basic human sensibilities—a sensibility that seems to glare and shine only in the birds of vermin, birds of prey like the vultures, crows, and scavengers. And the central fury of the rage comes from the disturbing diabolical question: "How could man ever justify the ways of God to man?"

The Wall of Mists

There is a universal axiom, an article of faith, that the mind of a man in forced solitary confinement sometimes takes on fluctuating bouts, vacillations between reality and fantasy, thesis/antithesis, affirmation/negation as he deals with his anxieties, frustrations, doubts, hopes, and even desires. It may be for these reasons that the prison wall, which at one time was sacred, now takes on a different symbol. No longer a symbol of the sacred and the profane, it now takes on the image of mists and those ineffable echoes that bring nothing but sadness to the mind of a lonely man. In this wall of mists and echoes, these condemned men seemed to celebrate with that awful, high-pitched, shrill laughter. They "feed no fires," "prompt no pains," and "wake no memories" because for them "Walls are the tomb of longing." As a reader trails this progression of thought in the poet's mind, he can begin to sense that the poet's mind seems to degenerate into fantasies of a witch Sabbath with all their horrifying orgies.

> Witches Sabbath what you hold
> Vermilion lizards in sun orgies
> Monster beetles in wall ulcers, broiled
> In steam of mildew drying
> Mists of metamorphosis
> Men to swine, strength to blows
> Grace to lizard prances, honour
> To sweetmeats on the tongue of vileness . . .

Here we witness the landscape of the physical content of the prisoners' cell which seems to be reminiscences of dungeons where witches celebrate on their Sabbath with deadly lizards in their sun orgies. We also see some monster beetles in the cracks of walls. A wall broiled in "steam of mildew drying." This wall really has become a wall of mists. A mist of metamorphosis, mutation that changes men to swine and strengthen them to receive blows. It is a metamorphosis that changes the vileness on the tongue of humans to sweetness.

But in this dungeon, in this cell for condemned men, death sometimes comes swiftly and quickly. That may be why

> There rose shrillness in the air
> Grunts, squeals, crackles, wheezes
> Remainder membranes of once human throats
> A thunder crack in air—the whip
> Of circle calling home her flock
> Of transformations?

We witness here the anatomy of death by hanging, as we listen to the
shrill cries of the condemned on their last breath. A reader can almost
suffocate by just thinking of those awful grunts, squeals, crackles, wheezes
of a man with a rope tightening over his throat to end his life. The man
now dead must face the other form of his journey: a journey of transfor-
mation to eternity. It is in this transformation that Soyinka weaves a
metaphysical conceit from Greek mythology. In Greek mythology, there
is a story about a sorceress called Circe, who transforms her victims into
beasts, but is thwarted by Odysseus with the herb, moly, that is given
him by Hermes. With this metaphor of Circe and her magic, Soyinka
transforms the issue of hanging political prisoners into mythological pro-
portions. But the irony is that in case of Circe, the punishment of her
victims was temporary because their shapes could be reversed. But death
to the prisoners was concrete, permanent, and sadly eternal. It is because
of that logic of the concrete, permanent aspect of death that the rhetorical
question "If Circe is calling home her flock of transformations," seems
redundant because the question is buried deep in the rhetoric of the ques-
tion, so that the question itself may be the answer. Because what else
would Circe do except call home her flock of transformations, just as
death transforms the human into another transcendental realm to meet
his/her God?

In a sad tone of agonized moaning, almost a requiem, the poet real-
izes that the death of these men leaves nothing but "Echoes that roam of
disembodied laughter. Born on soiled streams, sound waves. On maze of
under wall gutters." It is the blood of the slain that flows in dark chan-
nels that seems to link all the bereaved. And the smell of death usually
attracts birds of vermin, birds of prey, of clarion like bats to witness
another sacrifice of death. These deadly bats are attracted to the bad
smell of incense, so that they celebrate in that deadly ritual with dark
shadows that look like vapors of "purple paste of sunset."

However, at this point, a reader of this poem must stop to ask the
question: Where is the rage in the poem? In "Walls of Mists" the sense
of rage can be easily perceived when a man is confronted by insurmount-
able problems so that his mind degenerates into fantasies and dreams.
These human sensibilities of the fluctuation of the human mind between
fantasy and reality, filter through this poem with drips and cadences,
particularly when we listen to those awful "high-pitched shrills" of laughter
of the condemned men. The mind then becomes dizzy with agitation that
could produce spells reminiscent of witches Sabbaths with all their gory

and disgusting rituals. This cadence of rage may simply intensify when one is deprived of any decent sight, except the sight of deadly lizards in their sun orgies and some monster beetles or subjected to watching the hideous sight of a "wall of broiled steam of mildew drying." This sense of rage can be driven to a bursting pitch as one listens to those heart wrenching screams, grunts, squeals, crackles, and wheezes of condemned men gasping for their last breath, before their death.

The strength of Soyinka's poetry is in his capacity to inflict a traumatic feeling on a reader through his choice of words, sometimes with their gory insinuations, his turgid use of details that petrify and so force a reader to enjoy the drama of this trauma, these spells like watching a horror movie. This is the kind of writing that forced Philippe L. Labarthe to pose the question: Can language be too ugly sometimes and so fails to signify? (*Labarthe: Poetry as Experience.* 14).

Chapter IV

Amber Wall

To fully understand this poem, it is necessary for us to wrestle with the meaning and understanding of the word "Amber." This means that we have to resort to definitions. And here we run into problems because according to Kenneth Burke, in his book *A Grammar of Motives* definitions never lead us to the thingness of things." Definitions only tease us with substitutions, similes, allegories, metaphors and catachresis. But for lack of a better option, we must embrace the meaning and definition of the word, "Amber" from *Webster's Collegiate Dictionary, 5th Edition*. Webster has several attempts at explaining the word. The first is that the word is "a mineral, a noun, which has a yellowish, to brownish translucent fossil resin. It takes a fine polish and by friction becomes strongly electric." "Amber," according to Webster is also "a color, reddish-yellow in hue, of medium saturation and high brilliance." And as an adjective the word denotes "made of or resembling amber, amber color (33)."

All these confused attempts at explanation raise several questions. So, from the noun, if "Amber" means a mineral with a yellowish to brown translucent fossil resin, what color has this fossil resin? Is it yellow or brown? The second puzzle is this: if the mineral takes fine polish and by friction becomes strongly electric, are we not drifting precariously, but innocently into alien territory of quantum physics, thermodynamics or electromagnetism? The third explanation in Webster is that the word as an adjective means "A color, reddish-yellow in hue, of medium saturation and high brilliance. The secondary meaning to this adjective is "Made of or resembling amber; amber color." At this point in the search for meaning, the human mind becomes dizzy with agitation and so, we are forced to stop somewhere to pick up a brand of meaning that "Amber Wall" means a wall with a brilliant red or yellow color." At this point, also, we must remember that the word "Wall" has undergone a muta- tion, or metamorphosis in the mind of the poet. It started as a symbol of the sacred and the profane (Wailing Wall) and now to a wall of fossil resin with reddish-brown color. The different symbols of this wall also seem to reflect the degree of the intensity of feeling, the rage in the mind of the poet about his incarceration. This starts from a period of abject despair and bitterness, to becoming a mental struggle, to a gradual less- ening of tensions so that now the poet can even afford to see some beauty even in this ugliness. It looks like for the first time, he seems to see the brilliance of a wall that has been there all along. It is because he seems to have settled into the routine of prison life that he could now see:

> Breath of the sun, crowned
> In green crepes and amber beads
> Children's voices at the door of the Orient.
>
> Raising eyelids on sluggish earth
> Dispersing sulphur fumes above the lake
> Of awakening, you come hunting with the sun.

The poet in a prison cell could now visualize the beauty of the sun's rays on "the green crepes" and the children with their beautiful beads with all their shrill voices. He could also in his mind visualize the beauty of the fog over the lake in the morning. This is a suitable time to go hunting in the morning because the sun is shining its beautiful, lofty rays on the tree branches. A beauty that could completely overwhelm anyone. And with this beautiful morning, it becomes really hideous that a human being should be locked up, caged in prison walls. This beautiful morning should certainly intensify some anxiety and fantasy in the mind of the detained:

> Fantasies richer than burning mangoes
> Flickered through his royal mind, an open
> Noon above that closed door.
>
> I would you may discover, mid-morning
> To man's estate, with lesser pain
> The wall of gain within the outer loss.

The morning raises fantasies in the mind of a man detained—fantasies as rich and beautiful as ripe mangoes. And so, paralyzed with despair, the poet wonders if anyone could ever understand the restive mind of a man in this sordid situation, away from the beauty outside the prison gate. The answer of course is that only the prisoner knows. The poet's fantasies now rise to a high pitch as he visualizes all the beautiful joys of the nightlife in clubs with all the associated thrills and dances—dances that continue in some clubs till morning. These fantasies can really show a reader the site of rage in the poem. The rage resides in the fantasies of a caged mind—a mind that roams and fantasizes. The freedom of the mind to roam and fantasize is beautiful, but painful when the reality of a sordid situation persists and never goes away.

Purgatory

To name a poem "Purgatorio" (Purgatory) immediately ignites in the mind of a reader the sense of a divine experience. Divine in the sense that in Christian theological enunciation, purgatory implies a delayed redemption of souls of the dead who are waiting half way to heaven because they have to fulfill certain rituals of cleansing, penance, purification, and purging to be given final access to heaven. The critical concern here is that these souls are guaranteed entry to heaven because they are placed far beyond the safety of divine reversal! But the crowd of prisoners waiting for trial in this mock "purgatory" do not have any of the guarantees of the blessed souls. This is because this crowd of prisoners is the hybrid of all kinds of criminals from the simple drug addict to the scoundrel. To make it even more doubtful, this trial was false in intensions and execution because the government wanted to display a "circus-like" trial calculated to fool the public by diverting attention from its flagrant injustices. That is why the trial becomes comical like a circus:

A circus comes to circus town
A freak show comes to freaks
An ancient pageant to divert
Archetypes of purgatorio.

This trial looks like a comic circus, a freak show to freaks, because the staging of the structure of the trial was comical as we can see from the cast. First, there is a surgeon and a row of prison guards who are really an observation squad. Then there is a judge who announces the commencement of the proceedings. And perhaps, more disgusting to the eye, are the stage props who are a crowd of naked prisoners with a pail to empty trash from treated wounds and spittle. This looks really like a freak show that would amuse only freaks because it is calculated to divert attention from the glaring injustice that had permeated the whole government fabric like a pervasive miasma. This poem uses another of Soyinka's poetic conceits, because here he comically evokes an aura of the divine, the sacred on the profane.

The profanity of the title of this poem can also be seen from the fact that even the prisoners on trial are the complete opposites, an antithesis of the souls in purgatory because:

> For here the mad commingle with the damned.
> Epileptics, seers, and visionaries
> Addicts of unknown addiction, soul mates
> To vegetable soul and gray
> Companions to ghosts of landmarks
> Trudging the lifelong road to a dread
> Judicial sentence.

Here we meet a gathering of people from Sodom and Gomorrah, sin City, with all kinds of criminals and social derelicts—from the epileptic, seers, visionaries to the addicts of unknown addiction. The lucky ones in this group may be pardoned. But the hard-core criminals will face the rope and the hangman. For them, hope is lost against hope! That is why death for some is certain. That is why their minds dissolve in "vagueness to give them a look empty as all thoughts are featureless before they plunge to that love abyss: Death." This pain of their frustrating trauma provokes the rhetorical question: "Had it there ended? Had it all ended, there even in the valley of the shadow of night?"

The answers to these questions are disturbing. Disturbing because of the redundancy built into the question in this sense: How else would the condemned die? Can death kill death? However, these crowded prisoners and their fake trial maybe saved if they had the luck and the sanctity of the persona in George Herbert's poem: "Redemption." "Redemption" is a poem of luck, sanctity, persistence, faith, and divine providence.

Having been tenant long to a rich Lord not thriving,
I resolved Lord to be bold,
And make a suit unto him,
to afford a new small-rented lease and canceled the old.

The persona in Herbert's poem has self-knowledge, faith, hope, persistence, and the blessing of divine intervention. But the crowds in this poem, "Purgatory," do not. However, the sense of rage can be modulated and controlled when one is watching a perversion from a distance. The advantage here is clarity of vision and reasonable judgment. But when this perversion is too close and personal, it tends to provoke bitterness. And bitterness blinds vision and good judgment. It is that sense of a blurred vision that seems to be inferred in this poem whose sole purpose seems to be to mock the judicial system in Nigeria. No one can, in good conscience, believe that all trials, whether political or civil, are freak shows with the coloring of a comedy of the circus. This is excessive generalization and poetic exaggeration. And generalization tends to suppress dissident voices, thereby provoking the master and servant syndrome, so that in an inverse ratio, the poet seems to mimic the very style and mode of enunciation that he criticizes. It is of interest to observe that George Herbert, the metaphysical poet, believes in the fatherhood of God to all living things, including man. That is why the persona in his poem searches for spiritual piety as a means of sanctification and salvation. But in most of Soyinka's poetry, the sense of the divine is evoked for ridicule or to demonstrate the hypocrisy of the moment.

Chapter V

The Vault Center

"The Vault Center" seems to evoke all the whispers and moanings of a mind in a state of surrender. A surrender to a haunting sense of exasperation because all that one could do in prison is look through the cracks of windows to see the morning sunlight and the wood-pigeon and the egrets soaring into the air with the freedom and power to get their food. Sometimes the egrets in their recessions seem to be displaying some religious rituals to some unknown gods.

It should be of interest to note that when we juxtapose the freedom, power, and capacity of these birds to that of a man caged in a prison cell, the paralyzing sense of helplessness becomes overwhelming. This sense of malaise, this paralysis, this helplessness can begin to take a toll even on the strongest willed humans. It is this paralysis that moves the poet to evoke a sense of self-pity in the last stanza:

> The days sift filters down
> And I, a shawl of gray repose
> Fine moves of air, gather dusks in me
> An oriel window, eye on chapel ruins.

Here one can almost feel his heartbeat, his pathos as he watches sunlight trickle in through cracks in the window and the poet, a renowned world figure, a man who would later win a Nobel Prize in Literature in 1986, sees himself degenerate to a common symbol of a rag, a shawl, peering through the window. The rage and frustration reaches a boiling point only to provoke the question: "How much pain can one human being take?" Maybe this human pain, this trauma, is what an African

writer needs to regain his conscience by denying himself so as not to
become a chronicler and post-mortem surgeon:

> When the writer in his own society can no longer function as con-
> science, he must recognize that his choice lies between denying him-
> self totally or withdrawing to the position of chronicle and post-mortem
> surgeon. (Soyinka. *The Writer in a Modern African State.* 20).

The Procession

"The Procession" is a detailed depiction of the anatomy of the ritual of
death by hanging. In this poem, Soyinka is not so concerned with the
pain of dying, but more with the hideous brutality of a regime that sys-
tematically and brutally destroys the citizens that should be protected.
The poem does not enjoy the transcendental motif that we read in John
Donne's "Mortification." Nor do we experience the tedious life of the
fall of man and the excitement and thrill in divine intervention that we
read in Henry Vaughan's "Corruption." But Soyinka possesses the sor-
didness in the depiction of the ugly through ugly language—a language
that comes close to the pornographic horror that we see in Andrew
Marvel's "To His Coy Mistress."

In John Donne's poem "Mortification," he shows us that as soon as
man is born, he prepares for death. But this death has a transcendental
motif with a plea for eternal life,

> "Yet, Lord instruct us so to die, that all these dying may be life in
> death."

That life in death in Christian theology refers to the movement of the
human soul after death to heaven. Henry Vaughan also has this theologi-
cal trail in his poem "Corruption." In "Corruption" the poet tells the sad
tale of the fall of man and the subsequent punishment. But, as if by
inspiration, the poet confounded by this loss, tormented by anxiety, frus-
tration, doubt, hope, and desire for heaven screams out:

> Almighty Love, where art thou now? Mad man sits down and freezeth
> on: He raves and swears to stir nor fire nor fan. But bids the thread to
> spun. I see thy curtains are closed down; thy bow looks dim, too, in
> the cloud. Sin triumphs still, and man is sunk below the center and his
> shroud:

But hark! What trumpet's that? What angels cries.
Arise! Thrust in thy sickle?

In this poem man, having lost God's love, turns on himself in self admonishing depreciation with the question: "Almighty Love, where art thou now?" This is a rhetorical question that the poet does not seriously need an answer because the answer to that question is buried in the deep labyrinth of the question. That is why the question itself may seem to be the answer. The obvious answer of course is that God's love is lost and gone. Now, man has to fend for himself. That is why "man sits down and freezeth on." That is why "Man raves and swears to stir, nor fire, nor fan," but at the same time continues on his life of perdition. And in self-pity and despair, man was rejected even by God. That is why when he looks up to heaven for help he finds that even in God's house, "thy curtains had closed down; thy bow looks dim, too, in the cloud." The real course for anxiety now is that because God has rejected man in his perdition, "sin triumphs still, and man is sunk below the center and his shroud." But something amazing and mysterious happens. The fact that man has fallen does not mean that God does not love anymore or that God has even lost his magnanimity. It is through this divine love that God sends his angels to earth to rescue man. The thrill, the excitement in this divine intervention is simply overwhelming as the poet expresses in "But hark! What trumpet's that? What angel cries. Arise! Thrust in thy sickle?"

Here we witness the revelries and celebrations of angels rousing man and pulling him out of his perdition. But one does not see any of these revelries from the angels accepting the souls of these condemned prisoners from Nigeria in heaven. Soyinka may adopt the styles of metaphysical poets such as conceit, wit, introspection, and meditation, but he does not seem to share their theological faith. The poem procession opens with, "Hanging day. A hollow earth echoes footsteps of the grave procession."

That announcement echoes to almost all ends of the earth with ominous reverberations. An omen that reverberates with dread and horror. A horror and dread that the earth accepts by opening its bowels to these pitiful prisoners as they walk to their death in the morning. And to make certain that the reader does not miss the enormity of this horror, the poet describes and paints an ominous picture of the physical appearance and the behavior of the prisoners. These men are blindfolded and prepared for the sacrifice so they do not need any prayers. They glance sideways with their eyes raised and never lowered. These are the living dead, even before their death. They are out of this world and out of life. And by visualizing the last moments of these prisoners, the heart of the poet, the prisoners and the reader will admit that these men have moved away from the present towards the future. A reader's heart beats with terrifying palpitations, dizzy with anxiety and fear as one visualizes and almost listens to the shocking but rhythmic chorus of the footsteps of death: Tread. Drop. Dread drop. Dead.

Those sinister footsteps, those echoes, those sounds are the languages of death. If death ever has any language, it is the language of people who have lost their capacity for life, capacity for language, so that the only language left for them is that involuntary echo. The echo of steps moving reluctantly to their death.

In a light mood for a sinister occasion, the poet reverses his language from the poetic to that of informal conversation. This creates an intimacy, a closeness, a communal response by society to a tragedy that is enclosed in poetic stanza. We witness this perplexed individual monologue in:

> What may I tell you? What reveal?
> I who before them peered unseen.
> Who stood one-legged on the untrodden
> Verge-lest I should not return?

What reveal? The question is redundant because there is nothing to tell and nothing to reveal since we are all witnesses to this sinister ritual of death. And by looking at these men, the poet remembers how close he had come to death like these pitiful fellows. His salvation was that he was lucky. That is why he wonders if he could empathize with the plight of these prisoners. A plight that not quite long ago he may have shared:

> That I can receive them? I that
> Wheeled above and flew beneath them
> And brought them on their way
> And come to mine, even to the edge
> Of unspeakable encirclement?

This conversation in a solitary monologue continues to move slowly to the climax, to the sacrifice of horror where five people were hanged:

"What may I tell you of the five bell-ringers on the ropes to chimes of silence!"

It is ironic, the poet insists, that one could preach justice or guilt in a country where the lawmakers are themselves criminals. That is why "far away blood-stained in their tens of thousands, hands that damned these wretches to pit, triumph." In this society, nobody is free of evil. The only luck is that we are not yet caught. There are thousands in the community that may be just as guilty as these unfortunate ones who paid the ultimate prize. The poet, seized with a rage for the justice system, falls into a ranting rage, where he sees nothing else in this world, but filth, decay, stench of decomposing compost heap, maggots, and smoldering decay, where the world seems like the "whitest sepulcher where outside is white but inside is smoldering with dead men's bones."

> Earth is rich in rottenness of things.
> A soothing tang of compost filters.
> Through yeasting seeds, rain-sodden
> And festive fermentation, a swellness,
> Velvety as mead and maggots.

This language is simply filthy, disgusting, and nauseating like the language of one straight from hell. Here language and meaning, language and thought in their simulation and even in enunciation seem to be so easily interchangeable. This is language and thought that is so ugly that they form an ugly body that refuses to live among us. Earth is rich in disgusting things, in "rottenness" like the disgusting stench of decaying "compost." It is devoid of any form of sweetness. But if there should be any form of false sweetness, it must come from "mead and maggots." This is the kind of language that moved Philippe Lacove Labarthe to pose the question: "Is some language not so ugly that it may fail to signify?" (*Poetry as Experience.* 14)

Soyinka's language, however, the use of the ugly to portray the ugly, is in line with the prescriptions of poetry from our ancestral poets: Aristotle, Horace, and even William Wordsworth. Soyinka writes like the Greek poet Homer whom Aristotle claims in his *Treatise on Poetry* "was the supreme poet in the serious style, standing alone both in excellence of composition and in the dramatic quality of his representation of life, so also, in the dramatic character that he imparted, not to invective, but to the treatment of the ridiculous (36)." The critic, Horace, had some decided ideas about good composition, quality of language and the role of the ideal poet. He claims in *The Art of Poetry* that

1. The foundations and fountain-head of good composition is a sound understanding. The Socratic writings will provide you with material, and if you look at the subject-matter, the words will come readily enough.
2. That the experienced poet as an imitative artist, should look to human life and character for his models, and from them derive a language that is true to life.
3. Poets aim at giving either profit or delight or at combining the giving of pleasure with some precepts for life (Horace, 90).

The romantic poet, William Wordsworth, defines poetry as "Emotions recollected in tranquility or the overflow of powerful emotions (Wordsworth. The *Preface to Literary Ballads.* 20).

It may be necessary at this moment to appreciate the mimetic ancestral poetic influences that Soyinka's poetry enjoys. Soyinka, like the poet Homer, stands alone among African poets, both "In excellence of composition and in the dramatic quality of his representation of life, so also, in the dramatic character that he imparts, not to the invectives, but to the treatment of the ridiculous (Ibid. 36)." From the critic Horace, we know that Soyinka understands the foundation and fountain-head of good composition. That is why in his poetic conceits, the metaphors or symbols that he evokes, are no longer mysterious because they can be traced back to their genesis like the "Wailing Wall" or "Purgatory." Horace also believed that a poet must select and use a language that is suitable to his theme and true to life. Soyinka does that. That is why the description of a hideous hanging is treated with a language that is so tediously disgusting to the point of the traumatic. And perhaps more important to Horace is that a good poet should write for delight and entertainment as well as to teach and even edify his audience. Soyinka is a serious poet who does not seem to have time for entertainment. That is why some of his poems also have severe built in sarcasm or ridicule because Soyinka really believes that the writer should be the conscience of his society and not a "post-mortem surgeon."

Chapter VI

Jean Toomer

Jean Toomer was one of the rising literary artists of the 1920s, on his way to eternal fame as a literary master, but forced himself out of that race because of his fear of being identified as a Negro writer. Yet, his poetry deals with the beauty and the noble dignity of Black slaves and disgust for the human humiliation of slavery in the American South. Some of his poems reveal transcendental tendencies as he called on God to alleviate the sufferings of Black slaves.

The poems treated in this text are not selected in the order of their publications, but because of their brotherly and organic flavor of rage for the system of slavery. Some of these poems include "Carma," "Georgia Dusk," "Conversation," "Reapers," "November Cotton," "Prayer," and "Song of the Son."

Carma

The poem, "Carma," appeals to the reader through the subliminal, the senses, imagination that transfers this rage to the visual in simulation. The reader does not just read the words on paper, but he/she is compelled by the harsh sounds of the words to feel and think only of an eerie situation. That eerie situation involves visualizing slaves working in a sugar cane plantation under steamy, hot, summer weather. The word "cane" itself is a muted metaphor with some significations. The "cane" could mean a sugar cane plant. It could also mean a "cane" used for beating slaves. But in the mind of the persona in this poem, the word "cane" is compounded to represent only instruments of punishment.

However, in dealing with the use of language in this poem, we must be reminded of the teaching of the great critic Horace. It was Horace who taught us that every great poet selects a language suitable to his theme, to enunciate that theme. That was why Aristotle praises the poet Homer for his mastery in the use of language. An examination of the little poem, "Carma," will place the poet Toomer very close in ranking to Homer, in his mastery of his craft, particularly his use of language.

> Wind is in the cane. Come along.
> Cane leaves swaying, rusty with
> 					Talk,
> Scratching choruses above the guinea's
> 					Squawk,
> Wind is in the cane. Come along.

In the poem, the wind comes as a relief to the sweaty laborers in the plantation. But this wind seems to offer no relief because it sways the harsh rusty cane leaves on the already sweaty tormented laborers, thereby exacerbating the discomfort. This sounds like language in simulation as we listen to that rough, crusty dreariness and the haunting sense of harshness of the weather. We are forced to combine our audio-visual human sensibilities to listen and see the cane leaves swaying from side to side "rusty with talk." A talk that sounds like "scratching choruses above the guinea's squawk." The agonizing discomfort from this poem comes not just from the meaning, but from the sounds, the harshness of those sounds, the dreariness of feeling, and the despair which makes a reader feel like the sounds are coming straight from hell.

Perhaps even more disturbing is the behavior of the persona in the poem. This persona, rather than running away, calls for more in "Wind is in the cane. Come along." The behavior of this persona should remind the reader of the haunting cry by the Greek Sybil in "I Yearn to Die."

Georgia Dusk

"Georgia Dusk," is a poem of sublime, solemnity with the sense of rage. It is visible, but controlled as the poet deals with the evening mood, the content/context of slave labor, the hilarious and yet dignified revelries of the slaves, particularly as they feed on the nostalgia of lost nobility: This lazy mood of the evening comes in:

The sky, lazily disdaining to pursue
The setting sun, too indolent to hold
A lengthened tournament for flashing
                          Gold,
Passively darkens for nights
                Barbeque.

A reader encounters this sleepy mood of slumber that hesitantly, but persistently filters through this stanza. We see this in the "Lazy Sky," which almost scornfully refuses to pursue the sun. And even the sun is too lazy to play with the sky so as to produce a beautiful sunset. That is why the sun, without any events, simply slides into darkness. From this lazy mood, the sense of rage begins to smolder in the second stanza as we meet:

A feast of moon and men and
Barking hounds,
An orgy for the genius of
The south,
With blood-hot eyes and cane-lipped
                          Scented mouth,
Surprised in making folk-songs
                From soul sounds.

We can feel the implied rage in the sense that a typical evening calls for fun and revelries from men, women, and children. But every evening in Georgia turns out to be a night of terror where we see men with barking dogs looking for some possibly lost slaves. Those slave hunters themselves with blood-hot eyes are as dreadful and menacing as the very dogs that they use for their search. But there is an irony and even sarcasm in the love/hate relationship of the South to their Black slaves. There is also a beautiful play here; a tussle between language/thought, event/language, goodness/evil which, seem to create combustive tensions calculated to intensify the ugliness of slavery. The tension from this twisted and bizarre irony is in that double negation, where the white man not only enslaves the Blacks, takes away their freedom, but ironically the white man also steals Black music to make their folk songs. This sounds like a man who hates what he really loves!

A reader encounters this ugliness of slavery in its very anatomy, the content/context of slave labor, with all its associated nuances. We see a farming mechanism which uses "sawmills, buzz saws" that ploughs down the hills and knolls to plant crops. We see the ugly smoke rising from the "pyramid sawdust" as it levels the fields.

But as we trail the rage in the slumber of the evening, through the ugly farming mechanism, we run smack into mitigating circumstances, comic relief. There is a mitigating circumstance to the rage, a comic relief as a reader encounters the hilarious and dignified revelries of Black people with their heart warming nostalgia of lost nobility. The lost nobility we see in the "men, with vestiges of pomp," "a race with memories of kings and caravans, high priests, an ostrich, and juju men," singing merrily in their labors on the plantation. This is a teasing nostalgia, a memory that seems to aggravate what is forever lost.

With this sight of revelry, the poet seems completely overwhelmed and so wonders how Black people could fend off their suffering and still find time to have fun even in their labor. That is why Jean Toomer, like John Donne, George Herbert, and Henry Vaughan (metaphysical poets), seems inspired to evoke a sublime spiritual invocation with transcendental implications in:

> O' singers, resinous and soft
> Your songs
> Above the sacred whispers of the pines,
> Give virgin lips to Cornfield
>   Concubines,
> Bring dreams of Christ to dusky
>   Cane-lipped throngs.

In this invocation, the appeal has double implications. One is an appeal that seems to recognize the sublime, sacred dignity of the singers. The other is that the poet is really appealing to God to recognize and bless these noble people who toil without complaining. But something beautiful and even sublime is also happening in the poem. There is a mutation here of the innocent, secular music of the slaves with the sacred music of the pines. This contact suddenly confers a divine religious experience on the music of the slaves, thereby evoking that mysteriously sacred aura of the sacred over the profane. This encounter seems to change the dialectics of the sacred and the profane to the point that the sacred would tend to neutralize the profane by conferring a religious experience and veneration on the music of the slaves. Through this invocation, the poet has promoted and moved the slaves and their anxieties, frustrations, doubts, hopes, and desires to the level of the divine, the transcendental, to God, Himself. The slaves seem to have become the synonym for the suffering Christ who bore his pains without complaining. That is why their song brings "a dream of Christ to dusky cane-lipped throngs."

Conversation

In "Conversation," the poet struggles to deal with the distasteful topic of the genesis of slave trade. Slave trade, the poet believes, started from the deceptive practice of the white man who often made the Africans drunk with hard liquor like rum and whisky and even sometimes with poisoned food to enable the white man to steal African children. This has been a universal myth about the genesis of slave trade. A myth peddled by people who want to make slave trade conscionable and even tolerable. This line of thinking levels blame and places full responsibility solely on the white man. It also frees the African of any culpable responsibility. But the frightening truth is that the African is perhaps more guilty than the white man. And perhaps the guiltiest culprit is universal human greed. Greed for money, food, wealth, and all other human pleasures needed or not. Also, to blame the magnitude of slave trade on rum and whisky presupposes that all the wine cellars in Europe at this period must have been emptied. But the real culprits of slave trade were tribal wars, political instability, and that monster: greed.

The poem opens with that mythical proclamation:

African Guardian of souls,
Drunk with rum,
Feasting on strange cassava
Yielding to new words and a weak
                    Palabra
Of a white-faced sardonic god-
                    Grims, cries
Shouts Amen, hosanna.

In this poem, the poet confronts two monster events that fractured African society and culture. One was that introduction of alcohol into Africa which weakened not only the moral, but the spiritual resistance. This means that with the moral and the guardian spirit weakened, the enemy could come into your camp and walk away with your children, animals, and wife. But what the peddlers of this myth forget is that every tribe in Africa has its own alcohol perhaps more potent and deadly in content than rum and whisky. The second event was that Spanish introduction of the cassava (food tuber like the potato) which contains deadly alcohol. The serious implications of these two events are that while the British used alcohol as their baits for slaves, the Spaniards used poisoned food and their religion. Therefore, Africa at this period was bombarded morally, spiritually, and economically and these enormous forces fractured Africa.

From Jean Toomer, we learn that the introduction of Christianity to Africa was not a friendly gesture. It came with deception, intrigues, and falsehood. Through deception, the Spaniards imposed a strange religion on native people and so turned the African into that proverbial hunter's dog that goes mad and turns on the master. "Jumbo! Jumbo!" I could almost hear my father's voice trailing into the distance as he pleaded with Jumbo (his mad dog) to let him go as Jumbo tore into his clothes and legs. The Spaniards therefore forced this "white-faced sardonic god" on the Africans and so forced them to praise and scream hosanna to what? How could one worship a god he does not understand? What happened to the indigenous African gods? Did they just disappear or were simply sold for this "sardonic white-faced" God?

Perhaps for comic relief, it may be necessary to explain that terrible tragedy of Jumbo, the mad dog. In traditional African society, the hunter and his dog are given the sole responsibility by the elders, the ancestors, the spirits of the land and even God, Himself, to hunt for the tribe—to keep the tribe alive! But for the dog to turn on its own master also means disobeying and turning against all the multiple powers of the land. The ultimate solution to Jumbo's dreadful behavior is death. But Jumbo is mad, poisoned by a vicious enemy! So would you blame Jumbo (the mad dog) or the man who poisoned the dog?

Chapter VII

The Reapers

The sense of rage in the reapers comes from observing the daily drudgery and pain of slavery—an institution that treats other human beings like mules who work from morning till night without pay or even recognition. And yet these slaves have this noble dignity because they approach their job with courage and even without despair. It is this kind of situation that desensitizes a man to a point where killing a rat while plowing the field is not even noticed. In a way the life of the rat is just as meaningless as that of the slave.

November Cotton

"November Cotton" is a prophetic, diabolical, and even mysterious poem. The mystery stems from the symbolic and the physical harshness of winter—a season of death where the vegetation and some animals die. But in this poem, something mysterious and even prophetic happens. The mystery is that the cotton crop that was supposed to die turns out to bloom. And the girls with brown eyes who are usually afraid to love, now love without fear. These two cases are mysteries with endless significations. A reader can only speculate and surmise. Speculate that if these miracles could occur in nature as well as even in love, then there is hope that one day, even by mere chance, slavery would end?

Harvest Song

The poem "Harvest Song" seems to tease a reader into thinking that it is a poem about happiness and joy—a happiness that comes from the joyful music of the harvesters. But this is just as misleading as T.S. Eliot's poem "The Love Song of J. Alfred Prufrock." A poem that says nothing about a love song, but instead only serves as a medium for Eliot to dramatize the wasteful life of a man who at the end of his life, turns around only to wish he had lived. The trauma, the pain, the frustration, anxiety, doubt, hope and even desire are the same in both poems. "Harvest Song" seems to insinuate a happy song that harvesters sang during their labor. If it were a song of joy, it would have been a lyric because a lyric would be more suitable to demonstrate sentimental trivia. But if it is a song at all, it is a requiem or a dirge for the dead. This is a narrative tale of suffering with a sense of rage that trails throughout the poem, particularly if we realize that the slaves harvested oats, corn, and wheat (food) and yet they were starved of food and even drinking water. They could not even taste the fruits of their labor. Their state of mind should remind the reader of the sailors in Coleridge's ancient Mariner who suffered a similar fate. The sailors in Ancient Mariner were scourged of taste for water. Water that they could not have even though they were sailing on an ocean, the biggest body of water. Their pathetic moaning should be quite overwhelming:

> Water! Water
> Everywhere,
> Yet, not a drop to
> Drink.

The beauty of "Harvest Song;" however, even in its depiction of the ugly, is in that yearning and craving for communal solidarity in suffering. A yearning that seems to suggest that the pain and suffering of slavery will become lighter if shared and acknowledged by many. That sense of communal solidarity in suffering evokes the poignancy of the last stanza:

> O' my brothers, I beat my palms still
> Soft, against the stubble of my
> Harvesting. (You beat your soft palms too.)
> My pain is sweet.

Sweeter than oats, wheat or corn.
It will not bring me knowledge of
My hunger.

In a tone of sober and sublime invocation, the poet evokes that spirit of communal suffering of the slaves. They are comrades in suffering. That is why when the poet beats his "palm against the stubble" of his "harvest," other slaves do the same. The music, the suffering and the agony here are intensified because these are muted in the totality of communal suffering. Tormented and humiliated therefore, the poet and the slaves become desensitized to physical suffering. That is why their bitter suffering turns out ironically to be sweet. The suffering of the poet and the slaves is now sweeter than oats, wheat, or corn because they have undergone a metamorphosis of suffering to a point where they are now non-beings. That is why physical pain can no longer touch them. If it did, it could not hurt them because the bitterness is now converted to sweetness. These people have now been transported from the human to the transcendental, moving gradually toward God, Himself. That is why no amount of pain can do any damage because "t will not bring me knowledge of my hunger."

Prayer

The poem "Prayer" is a reflection of what happens to a man who has watched human humiliation and extreme degradation. The trauma from such awful observations affects not only the human body but also the soul and even spirit. That is why:

My body is opaque to the soul.
Driven of the spirit, long have I
Sought to temper it unto the spirits
Longing,
But my mind too is opaque to the
                    Soul.
A closed lid is my soul's flesh-eye.

The poet moans that because of this trauma of human degradation, the body has become so thick and dark that it is no longer sensitive to the yearnings of the soul. This means that efforts to unite the body and the spirit have failed. And to compound things even farther, the mind, which should yearn and crave the soul, has stopped these processes. The soul also is blocked from communion with the body. The culprit here is the system of slavery in the South that succeeds to fracture the whole life of an individual from his body, soul, spirit, and mind. The fact is that all aspects of a person's life instead of acting in unity, now appear to be dancing to the tunes of different drummers. Man here is dead even in living. He is the living dead. And like McDonald's unpublished sermon, the poet and the slaves have given all and have no more to give because:

> I am weak with much giving.
> I am weak with the desire to give more.
> (How strong a thing is the little finger).
> (How frail is the little finger.)

Though the poet and the slaves have given all they have to the South, they are still bombarded by the enormity of demands of the South. But the frail human being can only take so much before he is completely crushed. The human being that is as frail as the little finger cannot carry any more of the burdens. So, to help alleviate the tedium of human suffering, the poet invokes the help of the holy spirits, angels and even God to the rescue because "My voice could not carry to you did you dwell in the stars, O' spirits of whom my soul is but a little finger."

In this plea to the angels for help, there is a built-in admonition and even indictment of angels and holy spirits who seem too far away in the stars to be sensitive to the needs and frustrations of man on earth. This is a desperate show of rage when a man is so frustrated that he doubts receiving help even from God who may be his only refuge.

The Song of the Son

This song is a requiem for the dead, a sad song for the agony of slavery. It contains a plea to Christ to pour his death in a song that will last forever in the valleys. There is also an appeal to the South to receive their prodigal son, the poet, back without recriminations:

> O' land and soil, red soil and sweet-
> Gum tree,
> So scant of grass, so profligate of pines,

Now just before an epoch's sun declines
Thy son, in time, I have returned to thee,
Thy son, I have in time
                    Returned to thee.

The poet appeals here almost like the prodigal son for the South to accept him back even though he despises their practices of slavery. He then becomes almost prophetic in his predictions for the slaves and the South. He believes and hopes that one day slavery will end and that there is even hope of redemption for the South because he believes that their atrocities are redeemable. But the South has to make the efforts to redeem itself. And in an invocation that has become a trademark for Toomer, he evokes the beauty and nobility of Black slaves: They are like "dark purple ripened plums." The slaves, tortured and humiliated but bursting in Pinewood air, pass before the tree, before it is raped. And contrary to popular opinion the poet in this poem accepts his blackness:

One plum was saved for me
One seed becomes

An everlasting song, a singing
                    Tree
Caroling softly souls of slavery,

What they were, and what they are
                    To me,

Caroling softly souls of
                    Slavery.

The poet in accepting his blackness in, "One plum was saved for me" also inherits the obligations and responsibilities that come with it. He has become the conscience of the Black race so he must tell the horrors of their plight at the mountaintop and also sing their music to whoever will listen.

Chapter VIII

Literary Whispers on Jean Toomer

Gayle Jones in her text, *Liberating Voices*, informs us of the literary ranking by Robert Bone in a remark that he made about Toomer in 1923. It is amusing to peer into the heart of racism to witness its literary appreciation of artistic performance. That is why we may be forced to muse and laugh with Robert Bone when he writes

> Stein and Hemingway in Prose, Pound and Eliot in poetry were threshing and winnowing, testing and experimenting with words, stretching them until they became the pliant instruments of a new idiom. The only Negro writer of the 1920's who participated on equal terms in the creation of modern idiom was a young poet-novelist named Jean Toomer. (70)

An examination of this remark calls for some commentary. It is of interest and even praiseworthy that Toomer was ranked among the best writers of prose and poetry of the century. We see in this ranking that Bone either out of omission, accident, neglect, outright negation or amnesia, inadvertently did not recognize the poetic talents of other budding Negro writers who would later make the biggest splash on the literary scene in America. He could not see the talent and the zeal of the founders of Harlem Renaissance: men like Langston Hughes, Claude McKay, Alan Locke, Countee Cullen, and W.E.B. Dubois. And ironically it was this forced recognition of Toomer as a Negro artist that drove him from literary performance. He just wanted to be an American and an artist.

But, if Bone was concerned with ranking and race, Saunders Redding in his text *To Make a Poet Black* was concerned with the artistic great-

ness of Jean Toomer's "Cane" and his love of the Negro. Redding re-
marks that "In 1923 came Jean Toomer's 'Cane,' a revolutionary book
that gave definitions to the new movement and exposed a wealth of new
material. A youth of 28 years, fresh from the South when "Cane" was
published, he held nothing so important to the artistic treatment of the
Negroes as racial kinship with them. Unashamed and unrestrained, Jean
Toomer loved the race and the soil that sustained it. His moods are hot,
colorful, primitive, but more akin to the spirituals than the sophisticated
savagery of jazz and blues (104)."

Redding, who is very warm in his portrayal of Jean Toomer's racial
and intellectual traits informs us that Toomer brought "definitions to the
new movement and exposed a wealth of new materials." That new move-
ment was the Harlem Renaissance and the new material that he brought
to the movement was his new unique poetic and prosaic talent. Redding
was also pleased that Toomer loved the Negro race and even the soil that
sustained it. But if he loved the Black race so much, one wonders why he
refused to be identified with the race. And why this prospect of an un-
avoidable identification with the Black race drove him from his literary
pursuit? Did he love what he hated? Redding also shows us that because
of Toomer's transcendental craving, he loved the Negro Spirituals more
than the "Savagery of Jazz and Blues."

However, unlike Redding who saw the rich contribution of Jean
Toomer to the Harlem Renaissance and a warm love of the black race,
Cynthia Earl Kerman and Richard Eldridge in their text, The *Lives of
Jean Toomer,* have more scathing remembrances of Jean Toomer's ra-
cial, spiritual and intellectual life:

> He declared a mystical attachment to the soil, yet seldom
> got his fingers into it. He was black and white and abdicated
> from both groups. He was a writer who renounced writing
> but kept on writing all his life. He consecrated his
> life to transcendental greatness, but in his last years,
> his situation evoked not admiration but pity and regret. (14)

Kerman and Eldridge show us the life of a man with divided loyal-
ties: a life of negation and affirmation—a life of utter despair and even
transcendental betrayal. We see the confusion and the tension in his ne-
gation and affirmation in the sense that he loved the soil, but he could not
bring himself to live as a farmer. Secondly, he was black and white, but
he abdicated both groups. So, he was a man without race, a mulatto

shunned by both races. A reed dangling in the wind? Here is a man who really loved what he hated. That was why he "renounced writing, but kept on writing all his life." And perhaps his greatest source of despair was his failure as a transcendental saint! But who could say that with good conscience? What do we know about death, without dying?

As if all these attempts at evaluations were not enough, Nellie Y. McKay in her book, *Jean Toomer, The Artist*, shows Toomer's nostalgia for dealing with the past and his vision for solutions of the future which made him assume the mantle of poet, prophet, and priest. There is a fusion here of enduring characteristics in the life of a man who wanted to be a saint. A fusion of these divine professions really excite nothing but transcendental insinuations in the sense that the office of the poet from traditional societies (Christian, Greek, and African) really is that of a divine elect who becomes the voice of God, Himself. The prophet plays the same role. And the priest has the enviable position of mediator between God and man. If Toomer assumed these divine roles, callings, then he must have been a living saint. But he really needed to die to be canonized. There is also this curious implication that he personally assumed these roles. In simple language, it was not handed to him. Toomer, in the case of the metaphor of the mantle, begins to look like Charleman the Magnificent, who placed the mantle (the crown) on his own head rather than allowing the Pope to do it. He did that for good reason because the man that puts the crown on your head also has the power to take it down.

In trailing McKay's narrative, we can see that Toomer's boldness in dealing with the mantle of his divine callings is also reflected elsewhere. It is reflected in his bold stance on race. And McKay portrays Toomer in a tone of mild indictment by claiming that the success of "Cane" was not followed because it would have forced Toomer into dealing with racial identities and that he was a visionary "who sought his answers and platform in the sky while at the same time forgetting the risk of his landing" (239).

However, in terms of Toomer's reaction to his racial identity problems, the judgment of rational posterity will surely be mixed. Mixed, because there are some who may see him as a martyr for standing his grounds on race and losing a chance of eternal fame—an act that makes him look (noble and dignified) like Shakespeare's Othello, "The Savage Indian who threw away a pearl richer than all his tribe." But there are some who would see him as a hypocrite who claimed glibly to love the

Black race while at the same time was unwilling to identify with Blacks. McKay's second indictment was that Toomer was a visionary who forgot the risks of his landing. McKay's remarks here are redundant because a visionary should not worry about his landing. That is why he is a visionary.

But, we find it rather curious that Toomer should combine these divine roles of (poet, priest, and prophet) and rather than getting praises and veneration from the society he was despised. He may have been born in the wrong place because in traditional African society, a diviner, the spiritual and physical ruler, is usually a priest, poet, and prophet. And this is a highly sacred, feared, and revered office.

However, in a reasoned evaluation of Toomer, George Kent in his text *Blacks and the Adventure of Western Culture*, saw in Toomer fluctuating bouts and frustrations in dealing with race, identity, and the role of the writer who has to meander through these sensitive societal nerves. And so Toomer left America with a sublime and yet brutal and even haunting question. That question was "Could one just be an artist without the color tag?" But how can one escape color since he was chosen by color?

It should be noted that Jean Toomer is not alone in his resistance to racial stigmatization of the literary artist. A young Nigerian poet, Christopher Okigbo did the same in the World Black Arts Festival in Darkar, Senegal in 1964. Okigbo was awarded the prize of the Best Young Black Literary Artist of the Century. Okigbo declined to accept the award on the grounds that he was uncomfortable with the title of the "Black artist." He believed that art should be art without the color stigma. He came back to Nigeria a hero for standing up to the universal colorless nature of art. But history is very cruel to heroes as it dealt with Okigbo. He was cornered during the Nigeria/Biafra War, which was a war that required that we make the choice to remain in Nigeria and be universal in outlook or take sides and fight for Biafra and be a candidate of a group, localized, and boxed. Confronted with this call, Okibgo floundered and stumbled. He took sides with Biafra, fought for Biafra and died in the battlefront. History had exacted a penalty by emphasizing that every human being belongs first to the group before the nation and the universe!

Chapter IX

Claude McKay and the Poetry of Fire

Claude McKay was one of the prominent members of the Harlem Renaissance, a Black literary movement that blossomed between 1920 and 1940. Some of the members of this movement include Langston Hughes, Alain Locke, W.E.B. Dubois, and Countee Cullen. Some of McKay's poems contain the fiery fire-and-brimstone flavor of an impassioned Baptist minister who is out to frighten his flock into submission to change their ways and turn to God. But before we get into the voices in his poems, let us track down some literary and historical voices that instigate a curiosity in his poems. These literary and historical voices include Maurice Blanchot's interesting and animating text *The Work of Fire*; Nietzsche's *The Death of Tragedy;* and the fiery temper of that mythical Yoruba god Ogun (the god of thunder and rain, creation and destruction, death and childbirth).

Maurice Blanchot's text, *The Work of Fire*, is interesting because of the passionate intensity of his ideas, but more so because of the translator's efforts at translation. The problem with translations has been treated by Heidegger in his *Poetry, Language, and Thought*, where he complained that translations always seem to destroy the spirit of the work. The translator of Blanchot's text had the same problems with the meaning and exactitude. He made a tedious but insidious effort in explaining the etymological significations of a simple word: Fire.

Mandell, the translator, claims that the original title of Blanchot's essay was "La part du feu," which translates as "the part of fire." But the word "part" has two meanings in English. One is the division of some whole and the other, a role as in a play. The word "part" could also convey membership, such as belonging to a political party. All these attempts at explanation imply that the title of the text has several interpretations, which include the role of fire; the work of fire; and the partisans of fire. However, the word *feu* (fire) has other interpretations that imply illumination, such as traffic lights, tail lights, and signal flares. The word fire also has other assorted meanings such as the warmth of human feelings, someone's prose style, or the frenzy of someone's piano playing.

Mandell claims that when we begin thinking of all the implications of fire such as the role of lights, signals, flares, the sight of lights, "we are in the speculations about illumination, work taking sides, destruction (because fire does destroy what it briefly illuminates)." In short, we are now in the business of the interrogation of the text. But when we add the phrase: "Faire la part du feu" (to cut a firebreak), to stop a fire or in metaphorical terms, to cut one's losses in business, we are grappling with etymology. And all these tedious etymological attempts at explication of a simple word (fire) should remind us of the inadequacy of translations.

McKay's poems sometimes embody these various nuances, labyrinths of insinuations about fire that Mandell attempts to explain in Blanchot's text. The poetry carries even more. It also carries some traits of Nietzsche's *The Death of Tragedy* and that fiery temper of Ogun, the Yoruba god of creation and destruction.

In the *Death of Tragedy*, Nietzsche discussed the aggressive and even violent tendencies of the Appolonian against the sublime but passionate intensity of the Dionysian, all of which helped to sustain the Greek tragedy. McKay's poetry contains some of these whispers of the Appolonian and the Dionysian vibrations which give his poetry its vigor and vitality. And as an African, I can almost listen to that fiery and violent voice of that mythical Yoruba god, Ogun, the god of thunder and rain—Ogun, the God of creation and destruction, the god of death and childbirth.

I shall attempt to interrogate McKay's poetry as the work of fire which includes poems like "If We Must Die," "To the White Fiends," "Africa," "America," "Enslaved," "The White House," and "Outcast". I will compare the poetic temper in McKay's poetry with that of Wole Soyinka's poem, "Abiku;" W.B. Yeats' "1916 Easter Heroes;" and

Jonathan Edwards's "Sinners in the Hands of an Angry God." My first impulse is to begin with the poem "If We Must Die."

In the above poem, we encounter a combustion, mutation, or synthesis of all the attributes of fire that illuminates briefly before it destroys, the Appolonian aggressiveness, the Dionysian passionate intensity, and even the fiery temper of the mythical god Ogun, the god of creation and destruction. And as we approach the poem, we are forced to tremble because we are about to witness a brutal ritual, the sacrifice of fire:

> If we must die, let it not be like hogs
> Hunted and penned in an inglorious spot,
> While round us bark the mad and hungry dogs
> Making their mock at our accursed lot.
> If we must die, O let us nobly die,
> So that our precious blood may not be shed
> In vain; then even the monsters we defy
> Shall be constrained to honor us through dead!
> Oh kinsmen! We must meet the common foe!
> Though far outnumbered let us show us brace
> And for their thousand blows deal one deathblow!
> What thought before us lies the open grave?
> Like men we'll face the murderous, cowardly pack
> Pressed to the wall, dying, but fighting back!

This poem sounds like an impassioned voice of a Baptist minister inspiring his flock to turn away from their evil ways so as to avoid the wrath of God. McKay is here inspiring his followers to fight racism to death even though outnumbered. His maxim is that what really counts is not whether you die or live, but the courage you put into the fight. But the frightening part of the poem is in his use of language and the contagion of racism. His language shows the destructive contagion of racism in the sense that racism injures the victim as much as the victimizer. The damage of racism even on McKay is that, in his anger, in his fury, he forgot the logic of his own enunciation. The logic of avoiding dancing in the footsteps of the oppressor—the logic not to use his methods (violence in language and action) that will seem to mimic what he so forcefully condemns.

In the poem, McKay uses language meant for animals to refer to men. Black people are "hogs," while whites are "hungry dogs" and "monsters." This kind of language reduces even the victims and victimizer to the status of animals. The fight seems to degenerate to that of a "dog-eat-dog" morality that highlights the destructive effects of racism. This is poetry as fire that illuminates before it destroys.

McKay, however, is not alone in his concern for his people. His feelings can be compared to those of W.B. Yeat's suppressed anger and frustration for Irish Nationalists who were executed in 1916. On Easter Sunday, 1916, Irish Nationalists launched a heroic but unsuccessful revolt against the British government. A week of street fighting following what has come to be known as: Easter Rebellion. A number of nationalists were executed. That is why the poetic fury, anger, a burning fire and frustration in McKay has some kindred spirit (a relationship) with Yeats. And though tried as Yeats did, he still could not suppress his frustration and even anger:

> What is it, but nightfall?
> No, no, not night but death;
> Was it needless death after all?
> For England may keep faith
> For all that is done and said.
> We know their dream; enough to know
> They dreamed and are dead;
> And what if excess of love
> Bewildered them till they died?
> I will write it out in a verse—
> McDonough and McBride and Connolly
> And Pearse
> Now and in time to be
> Whenever green is worn
> Are changed, changed utterly:
> A terrible beauty is born.

Here is a story of anxiety. An anxiety of a man blinded by frustration and disturbed by a mind muddled to a point where he unleashes rhetorical questions. Questions that he does not seriously require answers to because the answers are buried in the dark labyrinths of questions, so that the questions themselves may be the answers. In the sentence "What is it but nightfall?" The answer would be easy if death were like nightfall because it would eventually lead to the dawn. Death in this case would simply be temporal. But it is not! Death is concrete, eternal, and sadly permanent. And the question "Was it needless death after all?" Defeats any form of answers depending on whether you were English or Irish. To the English, the death of these Irish national heroes was needless because their insurrection failed. But for the Irish, it was worth it because these heroes offered their ultimate sacrifice (their blood) so that a nation may be born. Yeats believed, however, that England gained nothing by these killings. In fact, by killing these Irish heroes, England inadvertently energized the spirit of Irish Nationalism. It was like killing Jesus Christ only to unleash that powerful resonance of his ministry through Peter and Paul! The poignancy of the poem comes from "We know their dream . . . and what if excess love, Bewildered them till they died?"

The poet believes here that these Irish Nationalists are heroes because they dared to dream—dream and yet die for the love of a dream. That dream is a liberated Ireland! The poet at this point in the poem appears so soaked and almost intoxicated with emotions that he takes on a personal and intimate bond with emotions as well as a personal and intimate bond with the fallen heroes whom he seems to know by name: "McDonough, McBride, Connolly and Pearse." These four he canonized into the spirit of eternity in a metaphor of the green vegetables that will never die. They will never die (even in their death) because in their death, they changed into eternity and so unleashed "a terrible beauty" that "is born" in the greens.

W.B. Yeats and McKay share a common bond, a kindred spirit in that enunciation of their frustrations, anxieties, doubts, hopes, and even desires that afflicted their political programs. Yeats was concerned with the liberation of Ireland. McKay with the liberation of Black Americans. For both poets, poetry was a vehicle of fire, a fire that briefly illuminates before it destroys. McKay met his illumination, his epiphany, the kind of light that blinded Saint Paul on his way to Damascus, transforming him from a murderer to a saint in his poem "To the White Fiends."

In the poem "To the White Fiends," McKay seems to have gone through a form of transformation, a spiritual cleansing, a metamorphosis to a point where he abandons the brutality of an eye-for-an-eye. So he takes on a high moral path (almost Christ-like) to be the fire that burns so as to illuminate all hearts of darkness:

But the almighty from the darkness drew
My soul and said: Even thou shalt
Be light, while to burn on the benighted earth

Thy dusky face I set among the
White for thee to prove thyself of higher worth.
Before the world is swallowed up in the night
To show thy little lamp: go forth, go forth.

In this piece, we witness McKay's spiritual relevations, an epiphany in "Even thou shalt be a light." In this sentence, the word "even," loaded as it is with ominous implications/complications, denotations/connotations of the impossible, of negation, of the improbable, reveals the level of spiritual purification, a kind of purge that McKay had undergone.

The verse seems to be bursting with intense religious impulse, particularly when we realize that the poet "shall be a light" to "burn awhile on the benighted earth" so that his dusky face will "set among the white to prove himself of higher worth." Here we find a baptism of fire which changes a man from a morality of "dog-eat-dog" to a craving of piety and even spiritual sanctifications. And the command to "Go forth, go forth" is no longer a command to go and fight, but to go out for peace and religious conversion, to bring the lost sheep to the father's barn. This spiritual, emotional, and political conversion of McKay seem to show the level of his greatness among the members of the movement, particularly if we consider Pascal's profound wisdom in intimating that "One does not show one's greatness by being on one extreme, but rather by touching both at once, by filling up the entire space between (*Pensees*, 266)." We have seen McKay's greatness by touching his two extremes (violence and piety) at once and filling the spaces between with spiritual sanctification. But when this seeming poetic greatness is examined under the critical lenses of more delicate themes, McKay fails the test because of his lack of decorum, a delicate understanding of the filial sensibilities of good taste in dealing with subjects like Africa and America. This floundering can be seen in his poem "Africa." In the poem "Africa," the continent is treated as the ancient home, the cradle of civilization because she could boast of science, pyramids, and ancient treasures. But ironically, this ancient land has been a modern prize for European nations and like the Sphinx, Africa watched the world roll by with no apparent achievements and no progress. In desperation, the poet seems to ask What did Africa gain from this ancient glory? Nothing?

Yet all things were in vain
However and glory, arrogance and fame!
They went—

The darkness swallowed thee again.
Thou are the harlot, now thy time is done
Of all the mighty nations.

This poem sounds like a requiem, a despairing moaning from a man who has just lost a grandfather, the mighty elephant. The sound of despair resonates in "Yet all things were in vain, honor and glory, arrogance and fame!" In a tone of pain and even disgust, McKay scourges Africa in blatant degradation and outright insulting terms when he says "The darkness swallowed thee again. Thou are the harlot, now thy time is done, Of all the mighty nations."

As an African, what seems revolting to me is McKay's lack of artistic control, a sensitivity to the objects of his fury, a lack of self-examination, and perhaps a concern for history and even judgment by posterity. To refer to a whole continent as a "harlot" is not only revolting, but downright ignorant even in the most debased form of the norms of acceptable dialectics. At this point in the poem, McKay degenerates in a poetic judgment to the level of a common street brawler who has no concern for common decency. And perhaps, even more disturbing is his brazen amnesia, or a lack of knowledge of the history of Africa's troubles by his use of the awful word "harlot" to describe the continent. The nausea in his language comes from the ominous connotations/denotations of the words "The harlot." The harlot freely and voluntarily sells his/her body for money. But Africa was raped and plundered from the outcome of the Berlin Conference of European nations, when Africa was mercilessly partitioned and shared among European powers. This act is common knowledge that any rustic on the streets of Los Angeles, New York, or Chicago should have known. And even more revolting is the fact McKay seems to blame the victim of rape for somehow being responsible for the crime against him/her. How can this be? McKay seems to lack that artistic self-criticism. And as Roland Barthes remarked so wisely, "the great artistic masters are those who know when to 'cut' without perforating a text like Flaubert." The poet's blatant lack of decorum or that sensitivity to the language of his themes seems to lower his status as a great poet. A reader interested in the masters who are adept to human sensibilities even to topics that touched them personally must turn to Wole Soyinka and W.B. Yeats.

Wole Soyinka, a Nobel Prize winner in Literature in 1986, a political agitator, imprisoned several times by a military dictatorship, wrote a poem (a metaphor for a writer), which signals nothing else but resistance:

> My name is Abiku,
> I am the suppliant snake
> Coiled on your doorstep.
> Yours is the killing cry!

This piece hints a sense of courage because a courage of compulsive resistance resonates. But it is a resonance of human language in the service of human sensibilities. The snake, a metaphor for a writer, is a violent and hostile reptile. The name of the snake (a writer) coiled on the doorstep is used to provoke anxiety, fear, doubt, hope, and even despair. The anxiety that the writer, like the snake, can bite, keeps that compulsive spirit of resistance clearly in the face of the oppressor. There is a marriage here between language and the event, language and anxiety, language and anger, language and meaning, all of which seem to be so interchangeable. The beauty of this piece, however, comes from that metaphoric conceit about a snake (a writer) that is "suppliant" (submissive, shy, feeble, feminine, and peaceful) but it is a snake that when provoked, can bite. And the deceptive ploy of being suppliant is used to draw the enemy in, so as to strike a killing blow. Since the snake, like the writer, is coiled on the doorstep (of the rich and powerful) and never goes away, that snake, as the writer, invariably becomes a tormentor, even of the oppressor.

The language of this small poem is purified and even sanitized, but it still carries the venom of a viper. McKay could also learn from Yeats's depiction of the fate of the Irish Nationalists who were executed because of their insurrection on that Easter Day of 1916. These Irish Nationalists led a rebellion that was crushed and the leaders executed. Some of these leaders (at least four) were personally known to Yeats. As an Irishman and a renowned poet, the incident of their death could have provoked Yeats to anger and even profanity. But not Yeats! His language on the subject is controlled, his tone modulated to unleash a poetic beauty in the birth of "a terrible beauty" that was born in the green vegetation. McKay lacks not only decorum, but his poetry is marred by other obsessive nuances: mood swings.

Apart from the lack of decorum, McKay's poetry suffers from obsessive poetic mood swings—from love to hate, from acceptance to rejection—which seem to make his poetry sound like juvenile street brawls. We see these mood swings in "If We Must Die" (a poem that advocates violence), to his spiritual conversion in "To the White Fiends," to a total lack of decorum and sensitivity in his depiction of Africa, a continent he insultingly labeled the "harlot." This mood swing, a confusion that hovers on the borders of a psychosis, is reflected in his poem "America." The mood here should recall the Appolonian aggressiveness against the Dionysian passion; that fiery temper of the mythical Yoruba god, Ogun (the god of creation and destruction). There are also traces here of Maurice Blanchot's fire that illuminates briefly before it destroys.

In the poem America, the poet catalogs all the ills that America has inflicted on him such as feeding him a "bread of bitterness," the choking "tiger's teeth in his throat," to "the negation of the breath of life." But shockingly, the next sentence, McKay opens with a sense of affection and love even for the very country that has tortured him:

> I love this cultured hell that tests my youth
> Her vigor flows like tides into my blood
> Yet as a rebel fronts a king in State,
> I stand within her walls with not a
> Shred of terror, malice, not a jeer.

Those nauseating verses provoke two critical concerns. One is that sense of a lack of a carefully drawn out thought process that warrants credibility. The other is the questionable sense of sincerity of his utterances. The real concern is this: How does he reconcile his seeming disgust for a dehumanizing system in one breath, while loving the same system in the next? And for good Christians, hell is a place they work hard to avoid. The question is How could he love a "cultured hell"? How does he enjoy that "vigor that flows into his blood from hell?" And in a voice that is so tamed that it amounts to a victim enjoying his own torture, McKay claims that "Yet as a rebel fronts the king in state I stand within her wall with not a shred of terror, malice, not a jeer." This verse is repugnant not only because the taming of the victim is complete, but because the victim now actually enjoys his own suffering. A maddening masochism!

However, despite the poet's profession of love for America, he still does not believe in the survival of the American civilization. That is why he claims that America's "might and granite wonders" will perish with time like those "priceless treasures sinking in the sand." This is a sad, fatalistic prophecy for a country he claims to love. These bouts of mood swings from outrage to sublime acceptance flow into the poem "Enslaved."

In the poem "Enslaved," the poet illuminates the Black man's alienation from the Christian West, while he is also disinherited even in Africa. And in a fit of rage, he screams out fire:

> My heart grow sick with hate,
> Becomes a lead
> For this my race that has no home on earth
> Then from the depths of my soul I cry
> To the avenging angel to consume
> The White man's world of wonders utterly.

This is a classic outburst of rage, of thunder and lightening for the suffering of the Black race, the dispossessed of the earth. The tone and temper of this piece is similar to Jonathan Edwards's "Sinners in the Hands of an Angry God." Edward used this sermon to frighten his congregation to submit to God. But they ran him out because of the fury of his sermon. This piece also contains a call to "Ogun," the Yoruba god of creation and destruction (the avenging angel) to destroy the white man's world utterly. The disturbing part of the poem is that Black people are not accepted even by the professed white Christians. But his anxiety and frustration seem misplaced because the poet claimed in the poem, "America," that "I stand within her walls with not a shred of terror, malice, nor a word of jeer." This is not the voice of a man traumatized by the brutal treatment of his people.

As a poet, McKay does not have a simply philosophic vision, a structured thought process or a systematic commitment to hate or love. His poetry shows splashes of emotional outbursts like a man who wakes up from a terrible nightmare only to fall into fits of suffocating bliss. We cannot compare his poetry to the sustained and well thought out poetic program of Langston Hughes or the brutal depiction of Black pain that one reads in Jean Toomer. Poetry, like all other forms of art, has its masters and mediocres. McKay falls into the second category: mediocre.

However, even mediocre poets have their respite, their moment of flickering light, their epiphany. McKay has that sudden vision. A vision that is sometimes sporadic, when the poetic muse shines light on him. That vision, buried in nostalgia for Africa, can be found only in one single poem that McKay wrote. That poem is "Outcast."

The poem "Outcast" expresses that nostalgia that torments every immigrant because of the pain of lost hopes, anxieties, frustrations, doubts, and even desires that seem to stop only in self-consuming cravings. The tragedy of the immigrant is in the fractured consciousness which makes going forward impossible, just as staying in his new country provokes only biting anxieties. This sense of alienation appears at first sight to be only local, but then it gains universal proportions because it is shared by all immigrants all over the world. It is the beauty of this universal craving and the sincerity of his thought that make this poem the most successful of all his poems. To substantiate this contention, let us examine the poem "Outcast."

> For the dim regions whence my fathers came.
> My spirit bondaged by the body longs.
> Words felt, but never heard, my lips would frame;
> My soul would sing forgotten jungle songs.
> I would go back to darkness and to peace,
> But the great western world holds me in fee.
> Something in me is lost, forever lost,
> Some vital thing has gone out of my heart,
> And I must walk the way of Life a ghost
> Amongst the sons of earth, a thing apart;
> For I was born, far from my native clime,
> Under the White man's menace, out of time.

Here is an expression of a longing that may be local, but takes on universal proportions. It is an expression of nostalgia for a homeland that seems to traumatize every immigrant. This is a sad tale, told in a tone of a lyrical nostalgia. The sad lyric of a "bondaged spirit" that longs for the dim regions (Africa). In a tone of agonized moaning, the lyric recounts all the unhealable losses such as language, song, and cultural dances of the tribe. Songs that though dimly remembered, yet bring solace to an afflicted soul. Though the poet escapes his sufferings temporarily into a song, this escape is a teasing adventure that usually bounces back into reality with crippling effect because "the great western world holds me in fee." The poem trails this sad tale into a poignant exasperation, a haunting sense of loss that because of its enormity must remain nameless:

Something in me is lost, forever lost
Some vital thing has gone out of my heart
And I must walk the way of life a ghost.

The above piece is the most heart-wrenching poem on nostalgia that I
have ever seen in print. The beauty of that piece comes from several
competing factions of loss. One is that sense of separation muted with the
conscious and the unconscious essences. Then there is that biting sense
of loneliness and alienation because he "must walk the way of life a
ghost." There is also that mysterious sanctity of the unknown that may
be menacing in its presence and even in its absence. This is the most
successful of all his poems. His depiction of nostalgia has a kindred
relationship with the novelist Milan Kundera and the critic Edward Said.

Milan Kundera, the Czech novelist, has been in self-exile in Paris
for at least 20 years, and Said has been away from Lebanon, his home-
land, since his youth. For Kundera, Prague, his home city, remains a
biting nightmare, a reminder of that loss which is as exasperating as it is
bewitchingly haunting. Here is the nightmare that Prague becomes for
Kundera:

> The same moviemaker of the unconscious who, by day, was sending
> her bits of the home landscape as images of happiness, by night, would
> set up terrifying returns to that same land. The day was lit with the
> beauty of the land forsaken, the night by the horror of returning to it.
> The day would show her the paradise she had lost, the night, the hell
> she had fled. (*Ignorance*, 17).

That passage tells the story of a mind wounded, traumatized, tortured,
and damaged to a point of destroying his sense of rational reasoning and
even his capacity to love what is worth loving: Prague. The images of
Prague that run through his mind are flickers of landscape, quick and yet
tantalizing, in their race through his mind. Something serious has hap-
pened to him. And like McKay, he is a walking ghost though he may be
living. But he is really a living dead. Something has happened to him, to
emotionally and psychically fracture his rootedness to Prague. His trag-
edy is that fracturedness which alienates him from Prague, while at the
same time making Paris an unbearable sanctuary.

This is the writing, however, of a novelist. And Kundera, the novel-
ist, romanticizes the crippling effect of estrangement from his home coun-
try. But when a man's feelings for his beloved homeland degenerates

into conflicting images of "happiness and terror," "beauty and horror," or "paradise and hell," then the psychological chaos in his mind would seem irremediable. There is a difference in taste and sensibility of expression, however, between a novelist and a literary critic. The novelist has a dual purpose of writing for entertainment with a little sprinkling of facts. But the critic looks for facts rather than entertainment.

If home for Kundera presents a tantalizing image, for Edward Said, the sense of loss inflicts irremediable damage to the emotional, intellectual and even spiritual life of the immigrant. Said presents that loss in very disturbing terms:

> Exile is strangely compelling to think about but terrible to experience. It is the unhealable rift forced between a human being and a native place, between the self and its true home; its essential sadness can never be surmounted...The achievements of exile are permanently undermined by the loss of something left behind forever. (*Reflections on Exile*, 173).

It is interesting to note that though Kundera and Said express a sad feeling of loss for their homeland, yet the magnitude of that feeling is slightly different. For Kundera, there is hope that one day the immigrant will return to claim his losses. But for Said, the damage is too terrible, permanent, and unhealable. His choice of words like "rift," with the connotation and denotation of "forcefully tearing" apart that can be a "terrible experience" that is not healable particularly because it is forced between a "human being and his natural place," between a "man's self" and his "true home," culminates in a terrible sadness that can not be "surmounted." Kundera and Said express the same longing and the crippling effect of a fractured life. But this condition does not have to be permanent because some immigrants do go home. The nostalgia, however, for the slave is different. Different in the sense that his desperate longing will remain just that, a longing with no hope of a return home. Trapped! It is in the depiction of this human condition, a human feeling that may be local, yet possessing a universal appeal, that makes "Outcast" the most successful of all McKay's poems.

In conclusion, the problem with McKay's poetry is shared by most members of the Harlem Renaissance, except Langston Hughes and Jean Toomer. That problem is the difficulty of trying to synthesize politics with literature without first understanding the individual or collective roles in each field. The result of this problem was that sometimes politics succeeded at the expense of literature. That is why some of McKay's poems could win political victories but lose aesthetic poetic marks.

The fire in McKay's poetry illuminates depending on the political climate. But this political illumination is usually done in bad taste and with a lack of decorum. His obsession with mood swings negates any form of philosophic vision such as a systematic commitment to love or hate. He does, however, achieve a trickling epiphany in the "Outcast."

Bibliography

Barthes, Roland. *S/Z. An Essay.* New York: Hill and Wang, 1995.

Bate, Jackson W. *The Burden of the Past and the English Poet.* Cambridge, Mass: Harvard University Press, 1991.

Bethel, Leonard Leslie. *The Role of Lincoln University (Pennsylvania) in the Education of African Leadership: 1854-1970.* Ph.D. dissertation, Rutgers University, New Brunswick, NJ, 1975.

Blanchot, Maurice. *The Work of Fine.*

Bloom, Harold. *The Anxiety of Influence.* Oxford: Oxford University Press, 1970.

Bone, Robert. *Cane.* New York; Harper Row Edition, 1969.

Burke, Kenneth A. A *Grammar of Motives.* Berkeley: University of California Press, 1969.

Coleridge. *Ancient Mariner in: The Anthology of English Literature.* New York: W.W. Norton Company, 1997.

Dorsch, T.S. *Aristotle, Horace, Longinus in Classical Literary Criticism.* New York: Penguin Books, 1965.

Eagleton, Terry. *Figures of Dissent.* London: Verso Press, 2003.

Eldridge, R./Kerman, C.E. *The Lives of Jean Toomer.* Baton Rouge: Louisiana State University Press, 1989.

Gideon, Charles. In (Jackson, Bate. *The Burden of the Past and the English Poet.* P.)

Heiddeger. *Poetry, Language and Thought.* New York: Harper/Row, 1971.

Jones, Gayle. *Liberating Voices.* New York: Penguin Books, 1992.

Kundera, Milan. *Ignorance.* New York: Harper Collins Publishers, 2002.

Labarthe, P.L. *Poetry as Experience.* Stanford: Stanford University Press, 1999.

Martz, Louis. *Introduction to Metaphysical Poetry.* New York: W.W. Norton and Company, 1973. John Donne, Herbert, Vaughan.

McKay, N.Y. *Jean Toomer, Artist.* Chapel Hill: The University of N.C. Press, 1987.

McKay, Claude. *An Anthology of African American Literature.* New York. W.W. Norton, 1997.

Nietzsche, Friedrich. *The Birth of Tragedy.* Toronto: Random House, Inc., 1967.

About the Author

Emmanuel Egar is an Associate professor of English at The University of Arkansas at Pine Bluff. He is the author of *Black Women Poets of Harlem Renaissance*, and *The Rhetorical Implications of* Things Fall Apart.